W9-ALL-256

Time for Outrage!

(Indignez-vous!)

Time for Outrage!

STÉPHANE HESSEL

Translation by Damion Searls

with Alba Arrikha

Foreword by Charles Glass

QUARTET BOOKS

CHARLES GLASS
BOOK

First published in 2011 by Charles Glass Books
an imprint of Quartet Books
27 Goodge Street
London W1T 2LD

Indignez-vous! was first published in France.
Text © Indigène éditions, décembre 2010
Translations © 2011 by Damion Searls,
with Alba Arrikha
Foreword © 2011 by Charles Glass

A catalogue record for this book
is available from the British Library

ISBN 978 0 7043 7222 1

Printed and bound in Great Britain by
T J International Ltd, Padstow, Cornwall

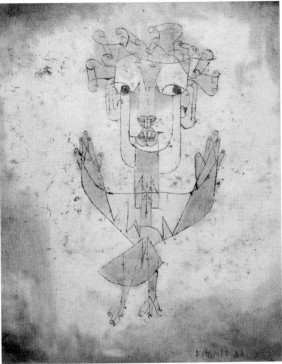

Paul Klee, *Angelus Novus*, 1920, 318 x 242 mm, The Israel Museum, Jerusalem

Stéphane Hessel refers in this book to a watercolour, *Angelus Novus*, by the Swiss artist Paul Klee and to the comments made about it by Walter Benjamin, the German philosopher, in 1940. Shocked by the German-Soviet Pact that led to the division of Poland and the beginning of the Second World War, Benjamin wrote about the watercolour in his *Theses on the Philosophy of History*. Walter Benjamin was the first owner of this work. To him, it depicted a repulsive angel, 'this storm we call progress'.

FOREWORD
Charles Glass

Towards the end of 2010, a small book by a ninety-three-year-old man unexpectedly reached the summit of the bestseller list in France. *Indignez-vous!* by Stéphane Hessel sold more than 600,000 copies between October and the end of December, propelling it over Prix Goncourt-winner Michel Houllebecq's novel, *La carte et le territoire*, by several hundred thousand copies. Stéphane Hessel had written other books. His publishers, the independent Indigène éditions in Montpellier far from Paris, had published other volumes. But none had reached the public in such numbers. The book anticipated the spirit of subsequent student demonstrations in France and Britain, as it did a wave of revolt that is challenging dictatorship in the Middle East.

Hessel's own life would make a novel, although his story is too hopeful to be told by nihilist Houllebecq. His father, Franz Hessel, was a German-Jewish writer, who emigrated to France with his family in 1924 when Stéphane was seven. Franz's friend Henri-Pierre Roché used him and his wife, the Prussian beauty Helen Grund, as models for Jules and Kate in his 1953 novel *Jules et Jim*. This was the enchanting tale of a woman who loved and was loved by two men that François Truffaut translated to the screen in 1962. Franz Hessel wrote novels in German and French. His admiration for France and French literature led him, with the great German-Jewish literary critic Walter Benjamin, to produce the first German translation of Marcel Proust's *À la recherche du temps perdu*. Stéphane grew up in a literary milieu that the German invasion of France shattered in 1940.

Having studied at the University of Paris's prestigious École Normale Supérieure, he served in the French army during the Battle of France and, like more than a million other French soldiers, became a prisoner of war. Following his escape from a POW camp, it took him six months to reach London to join General Charles de Gaulle and his small band of Free French *résistants*. His was a rare act of patriotism, when most of the French population professed loyalty to the Vichy leader, Marshal Philippe Pétain, and his policy of collaboration with Germany. The attitude of the majority of Hessel's colleagues in the military found expression in the decision of a French court martial that sentenced de Gaulle *in absentia* to death for treason. Hessel belonged to a tiny minority that was outraged enough to oppose Pétain's New Order that replaced 'liberty, fraternity and equality' with 'work, family and nation'.

While Stéphane was working with de Gaulle in London, Franz Hessel died in France. Stéphane parachuted into occupied France in advance of the Allied invasion of 1944 to organise Resistance networks. The Gestapo captured him and subjected him to the *baignoire*, a form of torture that would later be called waterboarding. He was transported to Buchenwald and Dora Concentration Camps, avoiding the gallows only by switching identities with an inmate who had already died. While being transferred to Bergen-Belsen, he escaped.

He became a diplomat after the war and was involved, along with Eleanor Roosevelt, in drafting the United Nations Universal Declaration of Human Rights. Awards and honours followed, the most recent of which were the Council of Europe's North-South Prize in 2004, the rank of Grand Officer of the Legion of Honour in 2006 and the 2008 UNESCO/Bilbao Prize for the Promotion of a Culture of Human Rights. Throughout his post-war life as a diplomat and writer, he retained the sense of indignation that drove him during the war. This book is a testament to his belief in the universality of rights, as his defence of Palestinians under Israeli occupation and of illegal immigrants in France attests. The popularity of this slim but powerful volume answered a public need for a voice to articulate popular resentment of ruling-class ruthlessness, police brutality, stark income disparities, banking and political corruption and victimisation of the poor and the immigrant. Hessel himself had arrived in France when many Frenchmen were decrying Jewish immigration as the 'threat from the East' (about which Joseph Roth wrote movingly at the time in essays that were later collected and published in the book *The Wandering Jews*). Of course, the real threat from the East was the Nazism that many on the French right admired as an antidote to what they perceived as the in-discipline of French society. Their intellectual heirs, echoing the earlier distaste for both foreigners and the ostensible fecklessness of the working class, hold positions of power in France today.

Hessel writes at the beginning of this book, 'Ninety-three years. I'm nearing the last stage in life. The end cannot be far off. How lucky I am to be able to draw on the foundation of my political life: the Resistance and the National Council of the Resistance's Programme from sixty-six years ago.' That programme, declared on 15 March 1944, set out the wartime and, significantly, post-war goals the Resistance was struggling to attain. Defeating the Nazis and their French collaborators was only a stage, the combined Resistance declared, on the way to the establishment of 'a true social and economic democracy'.

Hessel rejects the claims that the state 'can no longer afford policies to support its citizens'. It managed to provide that support immediately after the Liberation, 'when Europe was ruined'. How could it not afford to do the same after it became rich? Similarly, in Britain, the state paid for free universal education, including higher education, free universal medical care and other benefits that improved immeasurably the health and well-being of the country's children in the immediate aftermath of a war that left the country bankrupt. Now, after half a century of prosperity and the accumulation of fabulous fortunes, the British government says it can no longer pay for the social rights for which an earlier generation fought from 1939 to 1945 and for which it voted overwhelmingly in 1945. The new British coalition government's reductions in social benefits, its dramatic increase of the cost of university education, its transformation of the National Health Service into blocks of private trusts and its sale of community institutions like the Post Office to commercial enterprises come in tandem with its absolution of major corporations like Vodaphone from their tax obligations and its public subsidies to private banks. Outrage and indignation are not inappropriate responses.

Our politicians, guided by corporations and banks who rob the taxpayer when their business models fail, have revoked rights for which the anti-fascists struggled. To erode these gains in France, Britain and the other countries that fought alongside them against the Nazis and Imperial Japan is to reject the gift of the wartime generation's legacy. The countries that opposed the Germany–Italy–Japan Axis called themselves the 'United Nations' before they established the organisation of that name. American President Franklin Delano Roosevelt enunciated the Four Freedoms for which the American people were struggling: freedom of expression, freedom of religion, freedom from fear and freedom from want. Roosevelt's ideals found their way into the Universal Declaration of Human Rights:

> Whereas disregard and contempt for human rights have resulted in barbarous acts which have outraged the conscience of mankind, and the advent of a world in which human beings shall enjoy freedom of speech and belief and freedom from fear and want has been proclaimed the highest aspiration of the common people . . .

The conscience of Stéphane Hessel was outraged, as it had been during the war, whenever the post-war world betrayed the Resistance Programme and the Universal Declaration. In France, he found himself in the minority, as he had when he joined de Gaulle, when he demanded the right of Algerians to govern themselves. More recently, he has called on Israel to grant the Palestinians the right for which French men and women fought in 1944, for which Algerians struggled in the 1950s and 1960s and which Israelis claim for themselves: the right to self-determination and, thus, self-government and independence. To support those who seek this end, he has endorsed the Boycott, Divestment and Sanctions (BDS) proposal to sever economic collaboration with Israeli settlements, all of which depended on the removal of indigenous inhabitants and are illegal under international law, in the Occupied Territories.

In France today, Hessel calls on the young, many of whom have already marched through the streets with inchoate fury at President Nicolas Sarkozy's 'reforms'. They resent the balance Sarkozy is achieving between benefiting the banks while depriving the unemployed, the old, the students, the immigrants and the poor. Hessel's call for a renewal of the spirit of Resistance, albeit a pacific one, resonates in French traditions that immigrants embrace. It will do the same for youth in Britain and the United States, whom Hessel calls upon to remember their history and to defend its highest achievements.

Students at his alma mater, the École Normale Supérieure, invited Hessel to address them. Already popular with young people throughout France, he was likely to attract a full house. The authorities, supported by self-described intellectuals, intervened to prevent the meeting. Another, similar meeting was subsequently cancelled. Some credited those who censored Hessel with 'moral courage', but others came to his defence and to the defence of freedom of speech. Thousands signed petitions demanding that Hessel be permitted to speak, and thousands more are reading this book.

In London last year on the seventieth anniversary of de Gaulle's 'Appeal of 18 June' urging the French people to resist, Hessel said,

I was twenty-three in 1940 so, needless to say, those five years really had a huge impact on me. This is a war that I experienced in many ways: as a simple soldier in 1939 and 1940 before the French army's defeat, as a trainee in the Royal Air Force, as a Free French fighter working in the secret services in London, as a Resistance fighter in France, as a prisoner at the hands of the Gestapo and then as an inmate in two concentration camps . . . From this long and arduous adventure, something clearly emerged: the need to give a sense to my life by defending the values that the Nazis had scorned. This need led me to become a diplomat immediately after the war and to join the United Nations, where I helped to write the Universal Declaration of Human Rights.

Hessel's polemic echoes de Gaulle's words of June 1940, 'Must hope disappear? Is defeat final? No!'

The old Resistance fighter is battling those who would deny him his well-earned platform. Having taken on the Nazis, survived two concentration camps and kept his mind and spirit intact for ninety-three years, he should easily defeat Sarkozy's *fonctionnaires* and their apologists. The question before us is: Will we stand up to demand our own right to be heard?

Charles Glass, 2011

Time for Outrage!

The Legacy of 15 March 1944

Ninety-three years. I'm nearing the last stage. The end cannot be far off. How lucky I am to be able to draw on the foundation of my political life: the Resistance and the National Council of the Resistance's Programme from sixty-seven years ago. It is thanks to Jean Moulin[1] that all the elements of Occupied France – all the movements, the parties, the unions – came together within the framework of the National Council to proclaim their allegiance to Fighting France and to the only leader it recognised, General Charles de Gaulle. I was in London, having joined de Gaulle there in March 1941, when I learned that the Council had put the finishing touches to their Programme and on 15 March 1944 adopted it: a collection of principles and values for Free France that still provides the foundation of our country's modern democracy.[2]

We need these principles and values more than ever today. It is up to us, to all of us together, to ensure that our society remains one to be proud of: not this society of undocumented workers and deportations, of being suspicious of immigrants;

not this society where our retirement pensions and other gains in social security are being called into question; not this society where the media is in the hands of the rich. These are all things that we would refuse to countenance if we were the true heirs of the National Council of the Resistance.

After 1945, after that horrific tragedy, the forces in the National Council of the Resistance achieved an ambitious resurrection for France. Let us remember that this was when the social safety net that the Resistance called for was created: 'A comprehensive Social Security plan, to guarantee all citizens a means of livelihood in every case where they are unable to get it by working'; and 'retirement benefit that allows older workers to end their lives with dignity'. Sources of energy – electricity, gas, coal – were nationalised, along with the large banks, in accordance again with what the Programme advocated: 'returning to the nation the major means of production that have been monopolised, the fruits of common labour, the sources of energy, mineral riches, insurance companies, and big banks'; and 'establishing a true economic and social democracy, which entails removing large-scale economic and financial feudalism from the management of the economy'. The general interest had to be given precedence over particular special interests, and a fair division of the wealth created by the world of labour over the power of money. The Resistance proposed 'a rational organisation of the economy to guarantee that individual interests be subordinated to the public interest, one free of a dictatorship of established professionals in the image of the fascist state'. The Provisional Government of the French Republic (1944–6) assumed the task of realising this ideal.

Genuine democracy needs a free press. The Resistance knew this, and it demanded 'the freedom and honour of the press and its independence from the state and the forces of money and foreign influence'. Again, these goals were carried forward thanks to the press laws enacted subsequent to 1944. But they are at risk today.

The Resistance called for 'the practical opportunity for every French child to have access to the most advanced education', without discrimination – but the reforms proposed in 2008 run counter to this plan. Young teachers have refused to implement these reforms up to now, and I support their actions. They have seen their salaries reduced in retaliation. They got angry, they 'disobeyed', they decided that these reforms diverged too far from the ideal of education in a democratic republic, were too deeply beholden to a society of money and failed sufficiently to develop the creative and critical spirit.

All of these social rights at the core of the Programme of the Resistance are today under attack.[3]

Outrage Inspires Resistance

They have the nerve to tell us that the state can no longer cover the costs of these social programmes. Yet how can the money to continue and extend these achievements be lacking today, when the creation of wealth has grown so enormously since the Liberation, a time when Europe lay in ruins? It can only be because the power of money, which the Resistance fought so hard against, has never been as great and selfish and shameless as it is now, with its servants in the very highest circles of government. The banks, now privatised, seem to care primarily about their dividends, and about the enormous salaries of their executives, not about the general good. The gap between richest and poorest has never been so wide, competition and the circulation of capital never so encouraged.

The motivation that underlay the Resistance was outrage. We, the veterans of the Resistance movements and fighting forces of Free France, call on the younger generations to revive and carry forward the tradition of the Resistance and its ideas. We say to you: Take over, keep going, get angry! Those in positions of political responsibility, economic power and intellectual authority, in fact our whole society, must not give up or be overwhelmed by the current international dictatorship of the financial markets, which is such a threat to peace and democracy.

I want you, each and every one of you, to have a reason to be outraged. This is precious. When something outrages you, as Nazism did me, that is when you become a militant, strong and engaged. You join the movement of history, and the great current of history continues to flow only thanks to each and every one of us. History's direction is towards more justice and more freedom – though not the unbridled freedom of the fox in a henhouse. The rights set forth in the Universal Declaration of Human Rights in 1948 are indeed universal. When you encounter someone who lacks those rights, have sympathy and help him or her to achieve them.

Two Views of History

When I try to understand what caused fascism, the reasons we were overtaken by it and by Vichy, it seems to me that the rich, in their selfishness, feared a Bolshevik revolution. They let that fear control them. Yet all we need, now as then, is an active minority to stand up: that will be enough. We will be the yeast that makes the bread rise. Clearly, the experience of a very old man like me, born in 1917, differs from that of the young people of today. I often ask teachers to let me speak to their students, and I tell them: You don't have the same obvious reasons to get involved as we did. For us, resistance meant not accepting the German occupation, not accepting defeat. It was relatively simple. So was all that came next: decolonisation and the Algerian War. Algeria had to gain its independence. That was obvious. As for Stalin, we all cheered the Red Army's victory over the Nazis in 1943. Yet, when we learned about the Stalinist mass trials of 1935, it became necessary and obvious to oppose this unbearable totalitarianism. It was necessary, even if communism was a counterbalance to American capitalism. My long life has given me a steady succession of reasons for outrage.

These reasons came less from emotion than from a will to be engaged and get involved. As a young student at the École Normale Supérieure, I was influenced by Jean-Paul Sartre, an older schoolmate of mine. *Nausea* and *The Wall*, rather than *Being and Nothingness*, were important in the formation of my thought. Sartre taught us to tell ourselves: 'You as an individual are responsible.' It was a libertarian message. Mankind's responsibility cannot be left to some outside power or to a god.

On the contrary, people must commit themselves in terms of their personal, individual human responsibility. When I started at the École Normale Supérieure in rue d'Ulm in Paris in 1939, it was as a devoted follower of the philosopher Hegel. I attended the seminars of Maurice Merleau-Ponty. His class investigated concrete experience and the body's relationships with sense, with sense as meaning rather than as the five senses. However, my natural optimism, which wanted everything desirable to be possible, led me back to Hegel. Hegelianism interprets the long history of humanity as having meaning: that of mankind's liberty advancing step by step. History is made by successive shocks, of confronting and overcoming successive challenges. Societies progress, and in the end, having attained complete liberty, may achieve a democratic state in some ideal form.

There is, of course, a conception of history, which sees the progress of liberty, competition and the race for 'more and more' as a destructive whirlwind. That is how a friend of my father described history. This was the man who shared with my father the task of translating Marcel Proust's *Remembrance of Things Past* into German. I am speaking of the German philosopher Walter Benjamin. He drew a pessimistic message from a painting by a Swiss painter, Paul Klee, called

Angelus Novus [see page 5], which shows an angel opening its arms as if to contain and repel the tempest that Benjamin equates with progress. For Benjamin, who committed suicide in September 1940 to escape the Nazis, history meant irresistible progress from catastrophe to catastrophe.

Indifference: The Worse Attitude

It is true that the reasons for outrage today may seem less clear or the world more complicated. Who runs things? Who decides? It is not always easy to distinguish the answers from among all the forces that rule us. It is no longer a question of a small elite whose schemes we can clearly comprehend. This is a vast world, and we see its inter-dependence. We are interconnected in ways we never were before, but some things in this world are unacceptable. To see this, you have only to open your eyes. I tell the young: Just look, and you'll find something. The worst possible outlook is indifference that says, 'I can't do anything about it, I'll get by.' Behaving like that deprives you of one of the essentials of being human: the capacity and the freedom to feel outraged. That freedom is indispensable, as is the political involvement that goes with it.

We can identify two great new challenges:

(1) The immense gap between the very poor and the very rich never ceases to expand. This is an innovation of the twentieth and twenty-first centuries. The very poor in the world today earn barely two dollars a day. We cannot let this gap grow even wider. This alone should arouse our commitment.

(2) Human rights and the state of the planet. After the Liberation, I had the opportunity to be involved with drafting the Universal Declaration of Human Rights that was adopted by the United Nations on 10 December 1948 at the Chaillot Palace in Paris. It was in my capacity as chief of staff to Henri Laugier, Assistant Secretary-General of the UN and Secretary of the Commission on Human Rights, that I, with many others, was chosen to participate in drawing up this declaration. I will never forget the role played by Eleanor Roosevelt and René Cassin, commissioner for justice and education in the Free French government-in-exile in London and recipient of the Nobel Peace Prize in 1968, in formulating the Declaration. Nor can I forget Pierre Mendès France, a member of the UN Economic and Social Council, to whom we submitted our text before it went to the Social, Humanitarian and Cultural Affairs

Committee of the General Assembly. This committee included the fifty-four member states of the UN at that time, and I was its secretary. It is to René Cassin that we owe the term 'universal' rights, and not 'international', as proposed by our Anglo-American friends. For the real issue at the end of the Second World War was to free ourselves from the threats that totalitarianism held over mankind's head, and to do so, the member states of the UN had to commit to respecting *universal* rights. That is how to forestall the argument for full sovereignty that a state likes to make when it is carrying out crimes against humanity on its soil. That was the case with Hitler, who as master in his own house believed he was allowed to commit genocide. The Universal Declaration of Human Rights owes a lot to the universal revulsion against Nazism, fascism, totalitarianism – but also, thanks to our presence, to the spirit of the Resistance. I felt that we had to move fast so as not to succumb to the hypocrisy of victors promoting allegiance to values that no one had the intention of enforcing faithfully.[4]

I cannot resist the impulse here to quote Article 15 of the Universal Declaration of Human Rights: 'Everyone has the right to a nationality'; and

Article 22: 'Everyone, as a member of society, has the right to social security and is entitled to the realisation, through national effort and international co-operation and in accordance with the organisation and resources of each state, of the economic, social and cultural rights indispensable for his dignity and the free development of his personality.' Even if this Declaration has only advisory, rather than legal, force, it has none the less played a powerful role since 1948. We have seen colonised peoples refer to it in their struggles for independence. It fortified their spirits in the fight for liberty.

I am happy to see that NGOs and social movements such as ATTAC (Association for the Taxation of Financial Transactions for the Aid of Citizens), FIDH (International Federation for Human Rights) and Amnesty International have multiplied and become increasingly active in recent decades. It is clear that in order to be effective today, one has to act in a network and be connected in other ways, taking advantage of modern means of communication.

To the young, I say: Look around you, and you will find things that vindicate your outrage – the treatment of immigrants, illegal aliens and Roma people. You will see concrete situations to provoke you to act as a real citizen. Seek, and ye shall find!

Outrage over Palestine

Today, my strongest feeling of indignation is over Palestine, both the Gaza Strip and the West Bank. The starting point of my outrage was the appeal launched by courageous Israelis to the Diaspora: you, our older siblings, come and see where our leaders are taking this country and how they are forgetting the fundamental human values of Judaism. I went to Gaza and the West Bank in 2002, then five more times until 2009. It is absolutely imperative to read Richard Goldstone's report of September 2009 on Gaza, in which this South African judge, himself Jewish, in fact a self-proclaimed Zionist, accuses the Israeli army of having committed 'actions amounting to war crimes, possibly crimes against humanity' during its three-week 'Operation Cast Lead'. I went to Gaza in 2009, in order to see with my own eyes what the report described. My wife and I were allowed to enter thanks to our diplomatic passports, but the people accompanying us were not authorised to cross from Israel into the Gaza Strip or the West Bank. We visited as well the Palestinian refugee camps established after 1948 by the United Nations Relief and Works Agency for Palestine Refugees (UNRWA), where more than three million Palestinians (the 750,000 refugees driven from their homes in 1948 and their descendants, as well as those expelled in 1967), all of whom await a no-longer possible return. As for Gaza, it is an open-air prison for a million and a half Palestinians. In this prison, they must organise to survive. Even more than the physical destruction from 'Operation Cast Lead', such as the destroyed Red Cross hospital, it is the behaviour of the Gazans – their patriotism, their love of the ocean and the beach, their constant preoccupation with the well-being of their countless laughing children – that haunts our memories. We were struck by their ingenious way of facing all the shortages imposed on them. We saw them make bricks, as they lacked cement to rebuild the thousands of houses destroyed by the tanks. It was confirmed to us that there were fourteen hundred people killed on the Palestinian side – including women, children and the elderly – in the course of the Israeli army's 'Operation Cast Lead', compared to only fifty Israeli wounded. I share the South African judge's conclusions. For Jews themselves to perpetrate war crimes is intolerable. Unfortunately, history gives few examples of people who learn the lessons of their own history.

I am well aware that Hamas, which won the last legislative elections, was unable to avoid the launching of rockets into Israeli villages in response to the situation of isolation and blockade in which the Gazans find themselves. Of course, I think that terrorism is unacceptable, but we must recognise that when a country is occupied by infinitely superior military means, the popular reaction cannot be *only* non-violent.

Did it serve Hamas's interests to launch rockets into the town of Sderot? No. It did not serve their cause, but the gesture can be understood as coming from the exasperation of the Gazans. In this notion of 'exasperation', we have to understand violence as a regrettable consequence of an unacceptable situation. Terrorism itself, we might say, is a form of exasperation. And exasperation here is a negative term. What is needed is not exasperation, but hope. Exasperation is the denial of hope. It is under-standable, I would almost say it is natural. None the less, it is not acceptable, because it does not allow people to achieve the results that hope can.

Non-Violence: The Path We Must Learn to Follow

I am convinced that the future belongs to non-violence, to the reconciliation of different cultures. It is along this path that humanity will clear its next hurdle. And here, too, I agree with Sartre: we cannot excuse the terrorists who throw the bombs, but we can understand them. Sartre wrote in 'The Situation of the Writer in 1947', 'I recognise that violence manifested in any form is a failure. But it is an inevitable failure because we live in a world of violence. Even though it is true that recourse to violence to fight violence risks perpetuating it, it is also true that this is the only way to make violence stop.' To which I would add that non-violence is a surer way to make it stop. One must not support terrorists, as Sartre did in the name of this principle during the Algerian War and at the time of the attack on the Israeli Olympic athletes at the Munich games in 1972. It doesn't work, and Sartre himself, at the end of his life, ended by questioning the meaning of terrorism and doubting its justification. To say that 'violence doesn't work' is much more important than to know whether or not to condemn those who have recourse to it. In this notion of 'working', of effectiveness, lies a non-violent hope. If such a thing as violent hope exists, it is in the poetry of Guillaume Apollinaire ('How slow life is / And how violent hope is'), not in the political realm. In March 1980, three weeks before his death, Sartre admitted, 'We must try to explain why the world of today, which is horrible, is only one moment in a long historical development, that hope has always been one of the dominant forces of revolutions and insurrections, and how I still feel that hope is my conception of the future.'[5]

We must realise that violence turns its back on hope. We have to choose hope over violence – choose the hope of non-violence. That is the path we must learn to follow. The oppressors no less than the oppressed have to negotiate to remove the oppression: that is what will eliminate terrorist violence. That is why we cannot let too much hate accumulate.

The message of a Nelson Mandela, a Martin Luther King, is just as relevant in a world that has moved beyond victorious totalitarianism and the Cold War confrontation of ideologies. Their message is one of hope and faith in modern societies' ability to move beyond conflict with mutual understanding and a vigilant patience. To reach that point, societies must be based on rights whose violation prompts outrage – no matter who has violated them. There is no compromising these rights.

Towards a Peaceful Insurrection

I have noticed – and I am not the only one – the Israeli government's reaction to the marches each Friday by the citizens of [the West Bank village of] Bil'in, who do not throw rocks or employ force, to the wall against which they are protesting. The

Israeli authorities have described these marches as 'non-violent terrorism'. Not bad . . . One would have to be Israeli to describe non-violence as terrorism, and above all one would have to be embarrassed by the efficacy of non-violence, which works to gain the support and understanding of every adversary of oppression in the world.

The Western obsession with productivity has brought the world to a crisis that we can escape only with a radical break from the headlong rush for 'more, always more' in the financial realm as well as in science and technology. It is high time that concerns for ethics, justice and sustainability prevail. For we are threatened by the most serious dangers, which have the power to bring the human experiment to an end by making the planet un-inhabitable.

Still, it remains the case that there has been important progress since 1948: decolonisation, the end of apartheid, the destruction of the Soviet empire, the fall of the Berlin Wall. The first ten years of the twenty-first century, in contrast, were a period of retreat, explicable in part by the American presidency of George W. Bush, with 11 September and the disastrous consequences that flowed from it, such as the invasion of Iraq. We have had an economic crisis, but we have not initiated a new politics for economic development. Similarly, the

Copenhagen Climate Conference of December 2009 did not result in genuine political action to save the planet. We are at a threshold between the horrors of the first decade of the century and the possibilities before us of the decades to come. Yet we must keep up hope – we must always hope. The previous decade, the 1990s, brought great progress: UN conferences like that in Rio on the environment in 1992 and in Beijing on women in 1995. In September 2000, the 191 UN member states adopted the declaration on the 'eight Millennium Development Goals' initiated by Secretary General Kofi Annan, in which they agreed to cut worldwide poverty in half by 2015. My deep regret is that neither President Obama nor the European Union has come forward with what should have been their contribution to a constructive phase based on fundamental values.

How should I conclude this appeal to you to express your outrage? By recalling again that on the sixtieth anniversary of the Programme of the National Council of the Resistance, 8 March 2004, we veterans of the Resistance movements and the fighting forces of Free France from 1940 to 1945 (Lucie Aubrac, Raymond Aubrac, Henri Bartoli, Daniel Cordier, Philippe Dechartre, Georges Guingouin, Maurice Kriegel-Valrimont, Lise London, Georges Séguy, Germaine Tillion, Jean-

Pierre Vernant, Maurice Voutey and myself) said, 'Nazism was defeated, thanks to the sacrifices of our brothers and sisters of the Resistance and of the United Nations against fascist barbarity. But this menace has not completely disappeared, and our outrage at injustice remains intact to this day.'

No, this menace has not completely disappeared. In addition, we continue to call for 'a true peaceful uprising against the means of mass communication that offer nothing but mass consumption as a prospect for our youth, contempt for the least powerful in society and for culture, general amnesia and the outrageous competition of all against all.'

To you who will create the twenty-first century, we say, with affection,

TO CREATE IS TO RESIST.

TO RESIST IS TO CREATE.

Endnotes

1   Jean Moulin (1899–1943) was the Prefect of the Eure-et-Loire Department (Chartres) in 1940, when the Gestapo arrested and tortured him because he refused to blame Senegalese soldiers for a massacre committed by the Germans. After a failed suicide attempt in prison, he was released and resumed his duties as Prefect. His defiance of Vichy orders to dismiss all left-wing civil servants led to his dismissal. He escaped to London to join de Gaulle, who made him chief of all Resistance networks in occupied France. He returned twice to France to unite the disparate Resistance forces. The Gestapo arrested him on his second tour. The Lyon Gestapo chief, Klaus Barbie, tortured Moulin, who did not betray his colleagues. He died in Gestapo custody near Metz.

2   The National Council of the Resistance (CNR) was the underground movement created on 27 May 1943 by representatives of the eight major Resistance groups: the two pre-war syndicates, the CGT and the CFTC (Confédération Française des travailleurs chrétiens or French Confederation of Christian Workers), and six of the main political parties of the Third Republic, namely the PC (Communists) and the SFIO (Socialists). The National Council of the Resistance held its first meeting on the 27 May, under the auspices of Jean Moulin, who wanted to create the board in order to make the fight against the Nazis more effective and strengthen its legitimacy in the eyes of the Allies. General de Gaulle

ordered the CNR to devise a programme for the government, in anticipation of the liberation of France. This programme was passed back and forth a few times between the CNR and the Free French Republic, both in London and Algiers, before it was unanimously adopted by the CNR on 15 March 1944. The CNR formally presented the programme to General de Gaulle on the 25 August 1944, at the Hôtel de Ville in Paris, and it was published in the press the next day. One of the chief editors of the programme was Roger Ginsburger, the son of an Alsatian rabbi. Using the pseudonym Pierre Villon, he was general-secretary of the National Front for French Independence, a Resistance movement started by the French Communist Party in 1941 and one which Ginsburger represented from his permanent seat at the CNR.

3   Trade unionists estimate that we have gone from 75 to 85 per cent of taxed pension incomes to approximately 50 per cent. Jean-Paul Domin, senior lecturer in economics at the University of Reims, Champagne-Ardennes, has been writing about 'assurance maladie complementaire' (healthcare insurance) for the Institut européen du salariat (European Institute for the Salaried Sector). He reveals that, because society's most vulnerable cannot afford the premiums, they have chosen not to be insured. The core of the problem seems to lie with the fact that income is no longer in the domain of social policy. It was central to the edicts of 4 and 15 October 1945, when social security was endorsed and managed by unions as well as the state. However, Alain Juppé's 1995 reforms, followed by the 2004 law of Philippe Douste-Blazy (a politician who trained as a doctor),

resulted in healthcare being managed by the state only. Whereas, right after the Liberation, unionists controlled primary healthcare in every region, the President now nominates, by decree, the director-general of the Caisse d'assurance maladie (Health Insurance Fund), equivalent to the director of national health insurance. Today, union representatives serve as advisors, leaving the state, via its prefects, to run it.

4   On 10 December 1948, in Paris, forty-eight out of fifty-four member states of the United Nations General Assembly voted for the Universal Declaration of Human Rights. Six abstained: South Africa, because of apartheid, which the declaration condemned out of hand; Saudi Arabia, because of the inequality between its men and women; the USSR (Russia, the Ukraine, Belarus) and Poland, the Czech Republic and Yugoslavia, who all believed that the Declaration didn't go far enough in considering economic and social rights, as well as the question of rights for minorities. One notes, however, that Russia, in particular, was opposed to the Australian proposition to create an International Court of Human Rights charged with examining petitions addressed to the United Nations. Let us also remember that Article 8 of the Declaration introduced the principle of individual recourse against the state in case of violation of fundamental rights. This principle was applied in Europe in 1998 with the permanent creation of a European Court of Human Rights, which guarantees the right of appeal to five hundred million Europeans.

5   Jean-Paul Sartre and Benny Levy, *Hope Now: The Last Interviews*, University of Chicago Press, 1996, page 110.